REFLECTIONS
for teens

The Girl in the Mirror

michelle grover

JOURNEY FORTH™

Greenville, South Carolina

D0711800

Design by Jamie Miller
Composition by Melissa Matos
© 2006 BJU Press
Greenville, SC 29614
Printed in the United States of America
All rights reserved
ISBN 1-59166-507-8
15 14 13 12 11 10 9 8 7 6 5 4 3 2 1

Dedicated to
Mrs. Nancy Canedy,
one of the most praiseworthy women I know

Thank you for reflecting Christ so beautifully!

Contents

Her Relationship with God

Her Speech

Her Outward Appearance

Her Personal Discipline

Her Public Life

Her Private Life

Her Reputation and Final End

Preface

Dear Teen,

One summer while I was working at a Christian camp, I heard speakers week after week encourage the teen girls to study the two types of women in Proverbs. Do you know how many verses in Proverbs deal with women? A LOT! And tackling a project that huge may be a bit overwhelming.

So I've tried to make it easier by locating the verses for you. I hope that by having a study guide these truths will be brought into reaching distance for you.

Each lesson will include an "Opener," a "Focus Passage," a "Facing the Facts" section with questions to answer on the fact level, "A Closer Look" section with more thought-provoking meditations, a "Time to Reflect" section, an optional "Additional Study" section, and a "Memory Verse."

At the end of the guide, you will find tips on using some of the techniques you've learned in this study in your own personal devotions. That way, you'll be able to do a study like this one on your own.

Challenge yourself as you work through this study, but if it seems like you need more than one day on a lesson, I would rather you take your time and really grasp the truths instead of trying to swallow more than you can chew.

I hope you enjoy *The Girl in the Mirror*, and that, in the end, you will see God transforming you into a praiseworthy woman.

Sincerely,

michelle grover

Acknowledgements

I would like to say a word of thanks to each person that has influenced my life in pointing me towards God—siblings, pastors, teachers, friends.

Mom, you excel them all. And you've taught me so much! Thank you for being a role model worth following! I love you!

Dad, thank you for teaching me to be a woman that fears the Lord. Thank you for your love for Proverbs. And thank you for allowing me to use illustrations from our relationship in this study guide. I love you!

Alan, my wonderful husband, thank you for your help and encouragement throughout this project and my life. Your understanding of and love for the Word of God has been a constant prodding and challenge to me throughout the years that we've known each other, even before we were married. It is your heart for God that has so often rebuked me and stirred my heart to a truer love for God and His Word. I love you, Alan. Thank you!

And thank you to Mrs. Nancy Lohr and the staff at BJU Press for your encouragements and excitement about this project and for all your labors in the publishing process.

Truly all the thanks and praise goes to our great God and Savior Jesus Christ. "For of him, and through him, and to him, are all things: to whom be glory for ever. Amen" (Romans 11:36).

Introduction
Setting the Stage

This study could very easily be set up as a pageant comparing the two types of women in Proverbs. This pageant, unique to other pageants you may have seen or heard about, has only two contestants, but these two contestants represent all the women in the world: the praiseworthy and the problematic.

This pageant is **not** based on beauty; instead, it is based on character. We will be looking at both contestants through the "Mirror" of the Word of God, which perfectly reflects the true nature of all human beings.

You will be the judge of who wins the pageant.

At the same time, the spotlight will be on you, so be diligent in your study and honest in your reflections. In the end you will be glad you were. I promise!

Ready? Let's get going.

Lesson One
A Praiseworthy Relationship with God

Opener

Have you ever wished you could be a model? Thought it might be fun to at least try it out?

Upon consideration, have you decided that for some reason—the shape of your nose, the size of your lips, whatever—that you just might not rate?

Today, I want us to look at a model—unlike any you may have seen in a pop magazine or on TV though. No, don't worry about crash dieting or facelifts. This model is in the Bible, in our highlight book of Proverbs. Can you guess which chapter?

Focus Passage

If you guessed thirty-one, you're right! To start off, let's read Proverbs 31:10–31.

Facing the Facts

Before you throw in the towel and determine cosmetic surgery would be easier, thinking "I could never be like that," I want us to take a closer look.

What sticks out to you about this woman?

_____

If you're like me, it's all the amazing "stuff" she accomplishes. Getting up early, staying up late. No wonder! She couldn't fit it all in any other way.

Let's look at what this woman is like and take note of all the "stuff" she does. First of all, though, let's consider her title: the virtuous woman. What does the word _virtuous_ mean? (It's okay to use a dictionary.)

_____

How rare is a virtuous woman (verse 10)?

_____

How does she treat her husband (verse 12)?

_____

How does she do her work (verse 13)?

_____

What does she provide for her family (verses 15 and 21)?

_____

How does she treat others, including those less fortunate than herself (verse 20)?

_____

What two character qualities are her "clothing" (verse 25)?

_____

What does she do as she thinks about the future (verse 25)?

_____

What type of speech does she make a rule or law for herself (verse 26)?

_____

What is deceiving as to its worth (verse 30)?

_____

What is vain, empty, and temporary (verse 30)?

_____

What does she focus on rather than her own image (verse 30)?

_____

And is this woman praised (verses 28 and 30)?

_____

A Closer Look

I don't know how many times I'd read this passage before it finally hit me. Take another look at verse 30. In fact, write it out below.

_____

_____

_____

_____

This Proverbs 31 lady may or may not have been beautiful. But one thing is for certain—she had a healthy fear of the Lord. The truth of the matter is that she could not accomplish what she does apart from Him. You see, it's not about a good family upbringing, incredible physical training, an out-of-this-world IQ, or any of those kinds of things. No, the truth is, in order to accomplish what we should, each of us must **fear the Lord.**

Okay, so maybe you're thinking, That's nice, but what does _she_ have to do with _me_? She's married; I'm a teenager. Give me a break . . . and some time. Maybe someday I'll be like that, but not now. Are you _crazy_?

_Am_ I crazy? You tell me. Read Proverbs 31:1. Whose words are these?

_____

Okay, King Lemuel. But read it again. Where did he hear these words?

_____

Right. These are the words of his mother, the queen, instructing her son on the qualities to look for in a wife. And though a virtuous wife is described in verses 10–31, there are underlying characteristics that we as ladies, married or unmarried, should be striving for.

Read through Proverbs 31:10–31 one more time, but instead of just looking at the facts, let's take a closer look. In the chart, fill in the blanks with either the verse that exemplifies the quality or with the quality you see in the verse given. (You may even be able to find more that are not listed here.)

Verse	Quality
"The heart of her husband doth safely trust in her . . ."	Dependable, trustworthy, reliable
	Thoughtful, good, selfless
	Diligent
	Responsible, meets her obligations
"She considereth a field, and buyeth it: with the fruit of her hands she planteth a vineyard."	
"She stretcheth out her hand to the poor; yea, she reacheth forth her hands to the needy."	
	Wise
". . . in her tongue is the law of kindness."	

Verse	Quality
	Praiseworthy, deserving of praise, commendable
"... a woman that feareth the Lord ..."	

That last one—"a woman that feareth the Lord"—will keep showing up in each of the lessons on the godly woman in this study. You see, the only way to acquire the qualities that this woman possesses, the qualities that each of us are seeking to attain, is by beginning with the fear of the Lord.

So, what is the fear of the Lord? The Merriam-Webster dictionary gives several definitions of the word *fear*. Here are two of them. Circle the one you think the Bible is using in the phrase "the fear of the Lord."

1. "an unpleasant, often strong emotion caused by anticipation or awareness of danger"

2. "profound reverence and awe ..."

If you circled the second one, you're right! In fact, the rest of the dictionary definition is "profound reverence and awe [especially] toward God."

Time to Reflect

Apart from the fear of the Lord, the virtuous woman would not have been who she was. And apart from the fear of the Lord, you and I cannot be what we ought to be. Take some time right now to meditate on the truths we've been studying today, and answer the following reflection questions.

Do you fear the Lord?

_____

Do you love what He loves?

_____

5

Do you hate what He hates?

_____

Your answers to those three questions should all be the same, because all three are actually the same question restated three different ways.

As we continue our study, we will discover that the fear of the Lord is the crux of every contrast between the two women in this pageant.

Additional Study

You may want to look up the following verses if you would like to gain a fuller picture of what the fear of the Lord entails: Proverbs 1:7; 8:13; 16:6; 19:23.

Memory Verse

Proverbs 31:30

"Favour is deceitful, and beauty is vain: but a woman that feareth the Lord, she shall be praised."

Lesson Two

A Problematic Relationship with God

Opener

Have you ever been lost in the woods without a compass?

When I was in high school, my dad took up hunting as a new hobby. On his first big game hunt, he and "the guys" loaded up the pickup and drove through the night from Ohio to Colorado.

Late one afternoon, the guys tied up their horses and went to find good locations to wait for some unsuspecting elk to meander in front of them. After a while, they figured they had better check on the horses, so Dad volunteered to go.

Being an accountant and loving all sorts of math, Dad figured he would use some of his geometry skills and take the "scenic route" back to the horses. What he didn't factor in was the elevation changes on a mountain, a mistake that landed him on an entirely different plane without his bag—which contained food and water, a map, and his compass—and with only two bullets left in his gun to fire for help.

Darkness and cold were setting in, and Dad was getting pretty desperate. But to make a long story short, the Lord did answer Dad's prayers and allowed a hunter from a nearby camp to come into view and help him back to camp.

Today, we'll be looking at the second woman in our Proverbs pageant. This woman didn't just find herself lost, but actually *chose* to forsake her "compass."

Focus Passage

Read Proverbs 2:1–22, focusing especially on verses 16 and 17.

Facing the Facts

In this passage a father is giving his son instruction on sticking to the right path in life. In verses 2 and 3, what is the boy supposed to be inclining his ear toward?

_____

The idea there is of straining to hear every word even if that means leaning your ear closer to the one who is speaking.

What is the young man to apply his heart to (verse 2)?

_____

What is he to cry after and lift up his voice for (verse 3)?

_____

How are you supposed to seek for wisdom, knowledge, and understanding (verse 4)?

_____

If you seek wisdom, what will you come to understand (verse 5)?

_____

We focused some in our last lesson on the fear of the Lord. It is fairly simple to give a definition of what the fear of the Lord is; it is an entirely different thing to actually possess it. Rather than merely flipping through the pages of a dictionary, acquiring the fear of the Lord requires diligent seeking after wisdom.

Where does wisdom come from? Who gives wisdom to us (verse 6)?

_____

When will discretion and understanding keep you (verses 10 and 11)?

_____

Wisdom will deliver the son from what two types of people (verses 12 and 16)?

_____

Here is where we meet the praiseworthy woman's opponent in the pageant. How is this rival identified here (verse 16)?

_____

Identify the three descriptions of this wicked woman (verses 16 and 17):

1) the stranger which _____

2) which _____

3) and _____

A Closer Look

The first description deals with what?

_____

We'll come back to that in our next two lessons. The third description deals with her "forgetting" (choosing to forget) her marriage vow in order to pursue her own sinful lusts. For today's study, though, let's focus on that middle description. We are trying to establish this woman's relationship with her God.

"Which forsaketh the guide of her youth." What does it mean to forsake someone? (You can look up *forsake* in the dictionary, if that would help.)

_____

Read Psalm 48:14. Who is our guide?

_____

So, this wicked woman has *really* turned her back on whom?

_____

Does she fear the Lord?

_____

Do you think she devotes quiet time to God in the midst of her daily routine?

_____

Is there any reason to praise her?

_____

Is there any wonder this father wants his son to get wisdom and to be kept away from her?

_____

Time to Reflect

How is your relationship with the guide of your youth—with God?

_____

Are you spending time in His Word each day?

_____

Do you value quiet time alone with Him?

_____

Are you seeking after wisdom?

_____

Are there characteristics in your life that would make a godly father want his son to be kept away from you?

_____

Those are hard questions today. The truth of the matter is that we all need to be challenged regularly about keeping our personal relationship with God where it should be. But what a blessing it is to know that ours is not just a religion of dos and don'ts; ours is a personal, one-on-one, intimate relationship with the God of eternity: Creator, Sustainer, Redeemer, and Friend.

Additional Study

Remember, true wisdom comes from God. For further study, read James 1:5–8, 17, and 21–25.

Memory Verse

Proverbs 2:4–5

"If thou seekest her as silver, and searchest for her as for hid treasures; then shalt thou understand the fear of the Lord, and find the knowledge of God."

Lesson Three
Praiseworthy Speech

Opener

When it's your turn to pick where the family goes out to eat, where do you go? Do you and your friends have a favorite hangout for a pre- or post-game snack during volleyball season?

What is it that makes you like that place?

When it's my turn to pick, I almost always choose Chinese. Why? Because that's what appeals to my taste buds. True confessions: I *love* sweet and sour sauce.

Sweet and sour is a combo that actually works. But some "taste combinations" don't work in God's Book of recipes.

Focus Passage

Today's focus is actually not in the book of Proverbs. We'll be coming back to Proverbs before we're done, but our main focus will be in James. Read James 3:1–18.

Facing the Facts

James 3 discusses the struggles of controlling what?

_____

In verses 9 through 12, what ought not to be?

_____

In verses 11 and 12, James does a sort of play on words and switches from a human mouth to the mouth of a river or a fountain. What kinds of water don't mix?

_____ and _____

_____ and _____

As James continues, he goes straight from a discussion on speech into a discourse on wisdom. In verse 13, what word describes wisdom?

_____

Meekness can be a synonym for humility. Another way of looking at meekness is as "power under control." Wisdom controls what "no man [can] tame" (James 3:8)—the tongue. If you have godly wisdom, that wisdom "from above," what will your speech be like? Read James 3:17 again. Record the qualities listed below.

✓	Quality	Explanation
	Pure	Free from any dirty elements
		Not tending to stir up strife or disharmony; tending to promote peace
		Not rough, foreboding, or threatening
		Easily approachable, willing to listen to others rather than asserting your mind on the matter, people feel comfortable coming to talk with you even about a problem
	Full of	Kindness granted when unkindness seems to be deserved (mercy, not giving what is deserved)
	_____	

✓	Quality	Explanation
	Full of	Peaceable outcomes (see v. 18)
	Without _____	Not promoting just one side of the story, impartial, not prejudiced
	Without _____	Totally and completely honest, not hiding anything, not trying to make yourself look better than you are

Make that chart a spiritual checklist for yourself. Go through the characteristics one at a time, and ask yourself whether or not your speech is in line with God's wisdom. Put a check mark in the box if you are already making progress on that quality.

A Closer Look

With the background laid in James, it's time to open up our Bibles to the book of Proverbs and see what comes out when the people in Proverbs open up their mouths. Identify the characteristics described in the following verses.

Verses	Characteristic
Proverbs 8:7a	
Proverbs 8:8	
Proverbs 10:13a; 15:2a; 31:26a	
Proverbs 10:19; 13:3a; 15:28; 17:27a; 29:11b	Refrain, restraint, spare words, careful answer, keep in till afterwards
Proverbs 12:18b; 15:4a; 16:24	Health giving (to build up or strengthen), tree of life

Verses	Characteristic
Proverbs 10:32a	
Proverbs 11:16a; 22:11	
Proverbs 15:1a, 23, 26b; 16:24; 31:26b	Soft answer turns away wrath, joyful, good, pleasant, kind
Proverbs 15:23b; 25:11	

Read Luke 6:45. Where does what you say come from?

_____

Right! Whatever is inside of you will eventually come out.

What does the virtuous woman want in her heart (Proverbs 31:30)?

_____

If you have a proper fear of the Lord in your heart, will you desire to please Him in everything you say?

_____

Time to Reflect

Read Psalm 19:14. Copy this verse out.

_____

_____

_____

What does *acceptable* mean?

_____

Remember that acceptableness is one of the characteristics of godly speech (Proverbs 10:32*a*). Is this your heart's desire, that both your words and your thoughts be pleasing to the Lord?

What does the psalmist realize about Who God is in Psalm 19:14? What titles does he give Him?

If the Lord is your Redeemer, do you owe it to Him to speak the way He would desire?

If the Lord is your Strength, will He give you the ability to speak in a way that is pleasing to Him?

Additional Study

Look up the verses from the chart in "A Closer Look" that were already done for you. Personalize each passage and ask yourself how your speech matches up. Are you mixing bitter and sweet? Or are your words pure and peaceable . . . ?

Memory Verse

Proverbs 31:26

"She openeth her mouth with wisdom, and in her tongue is the law of kindness."

Lesson Four
Problematic Speech

Opener

Do you know the song "I'm a Little Teapot"?

If you're like me, you sang that song countless times growing up. I know of one Christian camp where, if you get three or more letters on any given day while there at camp, you have to sing "I'm a Little Teapot" in front of the entire camp before they'll turn over your mail.

Have you ever seen one of those old-fashioned teapots when the water begins to boil? Or maybe I should say have you *heard* one when it whistles that harsh, high-pitched squeal?

Proverbs 29:11 says, "A fool uttereth all his mind: but a wise man keepeth it in till afterwards." Another way to translate the word *uttereth* is *venteth*.

Have you ever heard someone say "I just needed to vent" or "I just needed to let off some steam"?

Have you maybe made one of those statements yourself? Or have you comforted a friend by saying, "That's all right. We all need to vent sometimes"?

Well, I've caught myself saying those things from time to time. I'd go on and on about something that I was disturbed about . . . letting off steam, so to speak. And then I'd feel bad because I knew I'd said too much and gone too far and often allowed my emotions to exaggerate something that really was fairly minor. The truth of the matter is, I'm **not** "a little teapot," and I don't need to let off steam. And no matter how emotional I get about an issue, if I'm wise, I'll hold my tongue. If I choose, instead, to "utter all my mind," I might as well scream as loudly and dramatically as the teapot whistles that "I'm a fool!"

Focus Passage

Read Proverbs 30:32. Copy it out below.

_____

_____

Facing the Facts

According to Proverbs 30:32, what should you do when you are tempted to brag on yourself or to let any evil thought in your heart leak out?

_____

Sometimes the best thing you can do for yourself is to literally put your hand over your mouth and force yourself to be quiet.

Where does Luke 6:45 say that our speech comes from?

_____

So what is in our heart when we are tempted to brag about ourselves?

_____

How does God feel about pride, according to Proverbs 6:16–17?

_____

Read Proverbs 12:18. What kinds of words are piercing like a sword?

_____

What should our words do instead?

_____

Proverbs 20:20 and 30:11 mention yet another problematic area of speech that is, again, rooted in pride. What is it?

_____

Cursing our parents is really any form of disrespect shown to them. It can be verbal or non-verbal communications, including shoving away, shrugging our shoulders instead of responding respectfully, or rolling our eyes.

A Closer Look

Let's go back to Proverbs and see what kinds of problematic speech are mentioned there. You'll want to read each of the passages in the sections because though they go together they may not use the same words. As you compare Scripture with Scripture, you will get a fuller understanding of the problematic area of speech being discussed. As you examine these verses, ask the Lord to show you any areas that may be problematic in your speech.

Verses	Explanation
Proverbs 2:16; 5:3; 6:24; 7:5, 21	
Proverbs 4:24; 10:32; 15:4; 16:28	
Proverbs 6:17, 19; 24:28b; 26:19	Lies, deceit, saying something and then recanting, "I was just joking/ kidding"
Proverbs 6:19b; 15:1; 16:28; 19:13b; 21:19; 24:2; 27:15	
Proverbs 7:11; 9:13b; 21:9; 25:24	

Verses	Explanation
Proverbs 10:19; 13:3; 15:2b; 29:20	Talks too much, pours out foolishness, hasty, doesn't think first

Time to Reflect

According to Ephesians 4:20–32, God's recipe for change involves putting off the old, renewing our minds, and putting on the new. In order to please the Lord in this area of speech, what kinds of speech do you need to put off (Ephesians 4:29 and 31)?

_____

Whom does wrong speech grieve (Ephesians 4:30)?

_____

What does your speech need to do (Ephesians 4:29 and 32)?

_____

What area of speech has the Lord targeted in your heart today?

_____

Remember, our speech comes from what's inside. Examine your heart. Is there anyone that you need to forgive? Is there anyone that you need to ask to forgive you?

_____

Will you determine today to speak kind and encouraging words that will minister grace to those who hear you speak?

_____

Will you determine to fear the Lord in how you use your mouth?

_____

Additional Study

Read James 1:19–21. What are Christians supposed to be slow to do (two answers)?

_____

What instead are Christians to be swift to do?

_____

"You have two ears and one mouth, to listen more and talk less"—there's some wisdom in that cliché.

Back in James 1:20, what are Christians to be working out, something that the wrath or anger of men does not accomplish?

_____

How do we learn righteousness (James 1:21)? What should we receive with meekness?

_____

Memory Verse

Proverbs 30:32

"If thou hast done foolishly in lifting up thyself, or if thou hast thought evil, lay thine hand upon thy mouth."

—OR—

Choose one of the other verses from Proverbs that the Lord is dealing with you about regarding your speech. If you choose that option, write the verse out here.

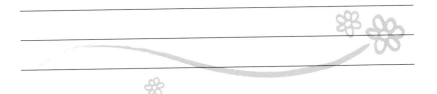

Lesson Five ✿ ✿
A Praiseworthy Outward Appearance
✿

Opener

I remember going to the store with my dad. We needed only three items, but Dad was sure he could remember without a list. He just decided to make up a little jingle . . . and then SING it . . . out loud . . . while we were in the grocery store. As a teenage girl, I was mortified! It's really the only time in my life that I remember my dad **really** embarrassing me. And I know it was only because of my pride. But still.

What embarrasses you? Can you remember the last time you were truly embarrassed? What was the cause?

_____

What would be the most embarrassing thing in your mind that could possibly happen?

_____

I can think of nothing more embarrassing than being, well, being . . . naked. It's bad enough to be seen in a "modest" swimming suit! But naked? Ugh. I can hardly bear it! I think it's a natural human tendency . . . now.

It wasn't always that way though. God created human beings without a need for coverings. But sin changed that immediately. As soon as Adam and Eve sinned, they became totally aware of their nakedness. And they, like I would, responded in utter embarrassment and with a desire to cover up! But there was no material, no sheet, and no clothes. All they had were fig leaves.

Focus Passage

Read Genesis 2:16–17, 25; and 3:1–21.

Facing the Facts

What had God commanded in Genesis 2:16–17?

_____

Did Adam and Eve obey (Genesis 3:1–6)?

_____

To summarize some of the details, the serpent (Satan) got Eve to question the significance of what God had commanded. Although Eve knew what God expected of her and Adam, the serpent was "more subtil" and convinced her to believe what would be pleasing to herself rather than to God. He first tempted her through her sense of sight, then through her intellect and pride. "And the eyes of them both were opened"—they woke up!

"And they knew" what (Genesis 3:7)?

_____

What was their first reaction (Genesis 3:7)?

_____

My main point today is not that they disobeyed; it is not that they tried to pass the buck and blame someone else for their sin; it's not even that they wreaked havoc on the entire human race by their sinning—though all of those things are true.

My point is that ever since sin entered the world, clothing has been necessary. And ever since clothing has been necessary, man and God have had different ideas about what is right in regards to properly covering the body.

What did Adam and Eve make their clothing out of initially (Genesis 3:7)?

_____

Was Adam and Eve's attempt to cover their sin sufficient?

_____

Like Adam and Eve, you and I cannot make a proper covering for our own sinfulness. What did God make clothing for them out of (Genesis 3:21)?

_____

Fig leaves and animal skins—very different fabrics, wouldn't you say?

On a side note:

In order to get coats of skin, an animal had to die. Before sin, there was no such thing as death. But as a result of sin, the Old Testament sacrificial system was established. In that system, animals had to die in order to cover man's sin. Ultimately, the sacrificial system was put to an end as recorded in the New Testament when Jesus Christ came and paid the penalty once for all on Calvary's cross. He died and rose again to conquer sin and death and hell. And if we by grace through faith place our trust in Him, we can be saved.

A Closer Look

So, is it possible for us to know what kind of clothing God approves of? Has He hidden His expectations for us? Or has He revealed them to us in His Word?

_____

Read 1 Timothy 2:9–10. Paul has just expressed his deep desire for men to pray. "In like manner also" could just as well be expressed, "I desire with just as much fervency." In other words, it is as important that ladies be modest as it is that men pray!

So what is **modest apparel**? R.C.H. Lenski in his *Commentary on the New Testament* gives some helpful insight on this passage: "Paul . . . here states that women are to dress in good taste."[1]

With shamefacedness: "Shamefacedness" (or "shamefastness") means being dressed in such a way that if the way I am dressed would cause anyone to think improper thoughts, I would be very quickly embarrassed—I would feel shame fast.

And sobriety: "soberness" or "self-control." Lenski says not using sobriety would include dressing for purposes of "vanity, pride, and other improprieties."[2]

Improprieties? What? Let's look at what Webster says about propriety (which would be the exact opposite of impropriety).

Propriety, *n.* 1. [Suitability]—*Syn.* aptness, suitability, advisability, accordance, agreeableness, recommendability, compatibility, correspondence, consonance, seemliness, appropriateness, congruity, modesty, good breeding, dignity . . .
2. [Conventional conduct]—*Syn.* decorum, good manners, good behavior, correctness . . .

Get the picture? See, it's not about dressing drably or out of style. Paul is not outlawing all jewelry. He's not banning ever braiding your hair. What he is forbidding is our drawing attention to ourselves rather than to the Lord.

Okay, so let's look in Proverbs 31 at the praiseworthy woman's clothing.

Do we know whether this virtuous woman was pretty?

Does it matter that we don't?

Remember, her attitude is that "beauty is vain [empty, worthless]" because her focus is on fearing the Lord. However, we do know that she did take care of herself and that she dressed nicely. Look up the following verses and note what you find about her clothing. The first one is done for you and is only implied, not directly stated.

Verse(s)	Characteristics of Her Clothing
Proverbs 31:11	Her husband can trust her to be appropriate, doesn't have to worry about her choices
Proverbs 31:13	
Proverbs 31:19	
Proverbs 31:21	
Proverbs 31:22–24	Silk, purple, linen: all very nice, not shabby
Proverbs 31:25	

And again, what is this woman's guiding life principle regarding clothing and every other area of her life (Proverbs 31:30)?

_____

Time to Reflect

Does it matter, in God's eyes, how physically attractive you are?

_____

Remember, God chose how you would look when He created you. However, **you** choose how you will dress. When you choose your outfit in the morning, whom are you aiming to please?

_____

Is how you dress appropriate for the activities that you participate in?

_____

Does what you wear make others want to trust your character (Proverbs 31:11)?

_____

Does your clothing communicate to others that you are pure and intend to stay that way?

_____

Do you fear the Lord regarding how you dress?

_____

Are there things you need to change regarding how you dress? Are there specific items in your wardrobe that would do well to be donated to charity, or better yet, the wastebasket in your closet?

_____

Commit to the Lord what you will change and be accountable to someone to really follow through with it. It's easy to make a commitment to the Lord and later try to reason your way out of it if you haven't gotten someone to hold you to it.

Getting rid of that favorite __(you fill in the blank)__ may prove to be difficult. The Lord never intended doing right to be easy. But doing right is always best. And as you become a woman that fears the Lord, He promises you will be praised.

Additional Study

You may want to look at 1 Peter 3:3–5 and Titus 2:3–5. And, as an extension of looking at 1 Timothy 2:9–10, think about this: As Christians, we are "professing godliness" (1 Timothy 2:10). What (in addition to "modest apparel, with shamefacedness and sobriety") are "women professing godliness" to put on (1 Timothy 2:10)?

_____

According to Matthew 5:16, what is the purpose of good works?

_____

Memory Verse

1 Timothy 2:9*a*

"In like manner also, that women adorn themselves in modest apparel, with shamefacedness and sobriety . . ."

Lesson Six
A Problematic Outward Appearance

Opener

As I prepared my scrapbook for graduation open house, I remember looking at my school pictures from fifth and sixth grade. "Mom, you let me go out of the house like *that* . . . on picture day?"

It seems like we all kind of go through those "geeky" stages; and for some reason (probably because they love us so much), our mothers tell us we look great.

But has your mom ever said, "Young lady, you're not going anywhere looking like that!"? Or has Dad ever ordered you back upstairs "until you find something decent to wear"?

Too much eye makeup, too short, too tight, too low—whatever the reason, it hurts. What we wear really is so tightly connected to who we are. When our clothing is critiqued, we take it personally, and understandably so. Maybe you were even trying to dress modestly and still either a parent or a teacher at school disapproved. That is not the time to lash back with excuses or justifications. Take a breath, and ask sincerely, "What am I missing?" explaining that you really do want to learn.

Modesty is a constant learning process. So don't get defensive if someone confronts you. Believe that he or she wants the best for you, that whoever it is is trying to protect you from harm. And seek to learn as much as you can from the situation.

Focus Passage

Read Proverbs 7:1–13, 22–27.

Facing the Facts

What kind of man is attracted to and fooled by this wicked woman (Proverbs 7:7)?

_____

Where did this simple one allow himself to be (Proverbs 7:8)?

_____

"Some explain 'her corner' as the corner near her house. Others see it as the corner to which she habitually came to lead others into immorality."[1]

At what time of day was this young man passing by her corner (Proverbs 7:9)?

_____

What problem does he encounter (Proverbs 7:10)?

_____

How is this woman dressed (Proverbs 7:10)?

_____

This woman may or may not have been a professional harlot, but she was setting herself up because she dressed just like one.

I remember watching a video in high school that gave all kinds of hints on getting better grades. One of the ideas that really worked for me was "Dress for Success." It really is true—you act differently based on how you are dressed. If you dress smart, you will often perform better academically. If you dress like a lady, you will more likely act like a lady. And if you dress like a harlot, you may eventually behave like a harlot.

I don't need to go into detailed description about what a harlot dresses like. But it is the type of attire that "attracts the young man's attention" as he approaches her.[2]

In a Christian Life Seminar at the WILDS Christian Camp in Brevard, North Carolina, Rand Hummel spoke about "the arrows of your fashion," and he urged teens to have them "pointing to your face." One group of girls, upon hearing this particular message, went to the craft shop, bought T-shirts, and painted arrows all over the T-shirts pointing to their faces. Obviously, that wasn't exactly what Rand meant, but you get the idea.

Continuing on in Proverbs 7, what do you think it means when it says that she is "subtil of heart"?

_____

Other words may be "cunning" or "wily,"[3] "crafty" or "devious." You see, how she dresses has a lot to do with what is in her heart. Just as we talked about the praiseworthy woman's heart fearing the Lord and thus producing positive outward effects, this problematic woman's conniving heart plays out not only in her conversation, but also now in her clothing and conduct.

A Closer Look

Read Proverbs 6:24–26. Is this "evil woman" beautiful?

_____

Is it wrong to be beautiful?

_____

But is it wrong to use your God-given beauty to attract guys to God-forbidden desires?

_____

Obviously, guys have a responsibility to keep their hearts (Proverbs 4:23) and not to lust after a girl's beauty (Proverbs 6:25). But, girls, we each need to be careful that we're not making it harder on them than it needs to be. You don't really want a guy to lust after you anyway. Wouldn't you rather he love you—and by that I mean love you in a God-intended way?

_____

As you walk through the mall or flip through a magazine, be watching for warning signs. Often the teen magazines and clothing departments are highlighting a look that is totally anti-Christian.

"You have to be different to make a difference." I don't know how many times I heard that preached as a high schooler sitting in chapel. And it is so true!

One more time, read Proverbs 7:10. "But I want to be accepted by my friends," "I want to look cool," "I like the way I look when I wear ___(you fill in the blank)___," etc. Ever struggled with those feelings?

"Listen, just 'cause I dress like this doesn't mean I'm gonna go do something dirty. I would never do something like that."

First Corinthians 10:12 states, "Wherefore let him [her] that thinketh he [she] standeth take heed [beware!] lest he [she] fall." *Wherefore* points back to what was said earlier. Read 1 Corinthians 10:5–12. Paul lists lusting, idolatry, fornication, tempting Christ, and murmuring as sins that previous believers fell into. "They are written for our admonition." Obviously, these believers thought they could handle the temptations. But did they?

_____

Was God pleased with them (1 Corinthians 10:5)?

_____

God will always make "a way to escape" (1 Corinthians 10:13), but we must be careful not to think we can escape temptations on our own.

Time to Reflect

Do you want to please God?

_____

Is it known of you that you want to please God? Is that your testimony (Hebrews 11:5)?

_____

If pleasing God means losing popularity, is it worth it?

_____

Do you have faith that God will reward you with things far greater than popularity if you will "diligently seek Him" (Hebrews 11:6)?

_____

Does your clothing reflect a heart that desires to please God or a heart that desires to please self and tempt guys?

_____

Will you commit to loving (in a Christian sense) the guys in your life and making it easier on them to keep their minds pure?

_____

Additional Study

Meditate on Psalm 90:17a: "And let the beauty of the Lord our God be upon us. . . ." That's the kind of beauty you want! Can there be anything more beautiful? Also, look at Psalm 96:9, in which holiness (set-apartness) is beautiful.

Memory Verse

Proverbs 7:9–10

"In the twilight, in the evening, in the black and dark night: And, behold, there met him a woman with the attire of an harlot, and subtil of heart."

Lesson Seven
A Praiseworthy and Problematic Personal Discipline

Opener

My volleyball coach in high school didn't want us to drink pop on game days because of how sugar gives you a quick energy burst and then drops you fast. My gym teacher wanted us to do really strange bends and stretches when we got to the aerobics unit. My track coach wanted us to stretch and run laps and drink lots of water. My math teacher expected homework to be completed and on her desk at the *beginning* of the hour. My piano teacher expected practice time to be recorded and theory pages to be filled in. And my parents expected me to keep my bed made, my laundry picked up, and my chores done. Why? Because each of them knew the value of personal discipline.

In today's lesson we'll be looking at both pageant contestants' personal discipline.

Focus Passage

Read Proverbs 31:13–27, 30–31.

Facing the Facts

Nothing is directly said about the problematic contestant's personal discipline, but we do know that in all other areas she sought to please herself, and we can assume that she would be no different in this area. If she did have any personal discipline, what do you think her motivation would have been?

We don't know for sure, since it's not specifically recorded, but I think we can assume the motivation would have been purely selfish.

On the other hand, we do have information recorded about our praiseworthy pageant contestant's personal discipline. We see her in several different venues. Note where she is in the following verses:

Verse	Where She Is
Proverbs 31:13	Seeking wool and flax at some type of market to buy material
Proverbs 31:14	
Proverbs 31:16	
Proverbs 31:24	Delivering girdles or goods to the merchants, perhaps down by the shipyard or in the marketplace
Proverbs 31:27	
Proverbs 31:31	

We don't know the layout of her town or how far she had to go, but she probably would've walked to get there. Now let's look at what she does.

Verse(s)	What She Does
Proverbs 31:13	Gathers materials
Proverbs 31:14	
Proverbs 31:16	Considers a field, buys it, with proceeds plants vineyard
Proverbs 31:19	
Proverbs 31:20	
Proverbs 31:22, 24	
Proverbs 31:24	Selling and delivering
Proverbs 31:27	Looking well to the ways of her household

And what time of day is she doing these things?

Verse(s)	Time of Day
Proverbs 31:13–27, 31	
Proverbs 31:15	
Proverbs 31:18	

A Closer Look

Now it's time to look a little deeper, not just at what she does, but at the character discipline behind her external discipline.

How does she work (Proverbs 31:13)?

_____

Does she have to be diligent in figuring out finances and household management (Proverbs 31:16)?

_____

Is the type of work she's doing physically easy?

_____

What two parts of her body are mentioned as being strengthened (Proverbs 31:17)?

_____

What two qualities are referred to as her clothing (Proverbs 31:25)?

_____

Does she sit around idly? Is she lazy (Proverbs 31:27)?

_____

What kind of work does she produce (Proverbs 31:18)?

_____

What does she receive in return (Proverbs 31:31)?

_____

Is it rewarding to be diligent?

_____

What is the main reason that she is diligent in her personal discipline (Proverbs 31:30)?

_____

Time to Reflect

Have you ever been accused of being a couch potato?

Do you do your work willingly?

Do you do your work happily? Cheerfully?

Do you make it a point to strengthen yourself physically?

Are you willing to work hard mentally?

Do you fear the Lord in this area of your life?

Additional Study

Read 1 Corinthians 6:19–20. Fearing the Lord in this area of our lives involves understanding and believing that our bodies are not our own—they belong to Jesus Christ. Do you live in the reality that your body is God's? Do you work at staying physically (and mentally) fit for His glory?

Memory Verse

Proverbs 31:17, 27b

"She girdeth her loins with strength, and strengtheneth her arms. She . . . eateth not the bread of idleness."

Lesson Eight
A Praiseworthy Public Life

Opener

Wouldn't it be awesome if everyone in your hometown thought you were a wonderful, capable, godly teenage woman?

Amazingly, there was a woman in Bible times who gained a reputation amongst an entire city (in a rather short amount of time, actually) for being a praiseworthy woman. Do you know who she was?

Her name was Ruth. And when Ruth told Boaz that he was a near kinsman, basically asking him if he would marry her, his response was: "Blessed be thou of the Lord, my daughter: for thou hast shewed more kindness in the latter end than at the beginning . . . And now, my daughter, fear not; I will do to thee all that thou requirest: **for all the city of my people doth know that thou art a virtuous woman**" (Ruth 3:10–11, emphasis mine).

I'm sure it was not normal or favorable for a Hebrew man to marry a Moabite woman. But Ruth became an exception to the rule because as she followed Christ and feared Him in her life, she gained citywide recognition as a virtuous woman! Boaz had no fear of his good name being marred by marrying her. She had proven herself and was praised because of her character and conduct, her "own works" (Proverbs 31:31).

Focus Passage

Read Romans 12:9–21 and then Philippians 2:1–11.

Facing the Facts

Another word for "dissimulation" is "hypocrisy." What does it mean to "Let love be without hypocrisy" (Romans 12:9)?

_____

What are we to hate (Romans 12:9)?

_____

What are we to hold fast to (Romans 12:9)?

_____

How are we to behave towards one another (Romans 12:10, 13–21)?

_____

How are we to serve the Lord (Romans 12:11 and 12)?

_____

All of these things work together. In a sense, this list delineates what the Christian's life is supposed to be like.

Which verse in Proverbs 31 goes along with Romans 12:13?

_____

In Philippians 2:1–11, we have the ultimate example of Christian living. Who is our example (verse 5)?

_____

How does Paul tell the Philippian believers they can fulfill his joy (Philippians 2:2)?

_____

These four ideas all carry the idea of unity. Unity produces joy, not only for ourselves but also for others.

"Strife" is "selfish ambition" and "vainglory" is "conceit." How much of what we do is to be done through strife or vainglory (Philippians 2:3)?

_____

How are we to do things instead (Philippians 2:3)?

_____

What form did Christ take on (Philippians 2:7)?

_____

Since Christ humbled Himself, what has God done (Philippians 2:9)?

_____

A Closer Look

Now that we've taken a look at what Christianity is supposed to look like and at our example, Christ, let's turn back to Proverbs 31 and see how our praiseworthy woman applies these things in her life. Specifically, what is this woman doing outside of her home?

Verse(s)	Activity	Explanation	Selfish or Selfless?
13–14		She's looking for ways she can meet the needs of her family as well as others.	Selfless
16–17		She's out being a real estate agent for the good of her family. Then she's noted for planting a vineyard and strengthening her arm.	

41

Verse(s)	Activity	Explanation	Selfish or Selfless?
20			
24		Again, she's doing something for the good of her family.	

Note verses 11 and 12. Does her husband ever have to worry about her? About how she spends her time or his money, etc.? Now, obviously, we don't know her motives for every one of her actions. But why can we assume based on her life and the context of the chapter that her motives are pure (Proverbs 31:30)?

I think probably, in addition to the fact that she's being a blessing to those in need in a physical manner, we can infer that she is being a blessing in an emotional and spiritual way by means of encouraging words. Read Proverbs 31:26b. Do you think she's only speaking kindly inside her home? Or do you think she's also using her kind speech outside the home?

Time to Reflect

Do you think more highly of yourself or of others?

What can you do to be a blessing to your family and others outside your home?

_____

Will you choose to fear the Lord in your "public life"?

_____

Additional Study

You may find some extra exhortations to love and help others in Galatians 5:13–14, 22–23; 6:1–3. Note that love is possible only through the Holy Spirit's enabling.

Memory Verse

Proverbs 31:20

"She stretcheth out her hand to the poor; yea, she reacheth forth her hands to the needy."

—OR—
Galatians 5:13c

". . . by love serve one another."

Lesson Nine
A Problematic Public Life

Opener

"Where's the love, man?" Ever heard that from one of your friends?

What were they really asking?

If I read it right, most of the time, what they're really asking is "Come on, who you more interested in—yourself or me? Who's more important here?"

You know, when it comes right down to it, we're all pretty interested in looking out for "Ol' Number One"—that being ourselves. And why not? The philosophy is all over the media: "Gimme a break," "Have it your way," "Your way, right away," "Made for you," "Have you had your break today?," "You deserve it," "Just the way you like it." The list goes on and on. In fact you could probably name some of the companies that use those slogans. Be honest: did any of the jingles from the advertisements come into your mind?

We're bombarded with "YN-1" missiles—as I like to call them—every day, multiple times a day. What are YN-1 missiles? They're little missiles that attack our minds telling us "You're Number One." And they're really the fiery darts of the devil that he's using to try to convince us it's "okay" to be selfish . . . "just this once."

Watch as the battle rages and our problematic woman falls prey to all kinds of YN-1s.

Focus Passage

Read Proverbs 7:1–27.

Facing the Facts

"The bulk of the chapter tells of a young man's fall into the snare set for him by an immoral woman. The detailed description of the passage comes from Solomon's role as an eyewitness. He observes the couple when they think they are alone and have no reason to temper their language to meet social expectations. . . . From the nature of the narrative, it is likely that Solomon had observed the woman on several occasions. While he relates the incident as though it involves one particular youth, he adds details that have come from other occasions, e.g., vv.7, 9, 12"[1].

Where was Solomon observing from in Proverbs 7:6?

_____

How old was this woman's target man (Proverbs 7:7)?

_____

What time does this problematic, adulterous woman go out and about (Proverbs 7:9)?

_____

Where does she go (Proverbs 7:8, 12)?

_____

Why is she out at this time of night and in these places? What does she want?

_____

Who do you think she is primarily focused on pleasing: the young man, her husband, God, or herself?

_____

Does she get what she wants (Proverbs 7:13–23)?

_____

Do you think she is satisfied?

_____

Do you think she's happy when it's all over?

_____

Do you think her husband will be happy when he comes home?

_____

A Closer Look

This woman's reasoning is entirely selfish, and she has deceived herself into thinking she's only affecting herself. In fact, she believes that no one will ever know.

She then convinces the youth also that no one has to know. What is her thinking (Proverbs 7:19–20)?

_____

Read Ezekiel 8:12. What are the two lies a person has to convince himself or herself of in order to sin?

"The Lord _____ ;

the Lord _____ ."

In effect, "The Lord doesn't see me, and even if He sees me He doesn't really care."[2]

But what is the truth (Proverbs 15:3)?

_____

What can we be sure of in Numbers 32:23?

_____

Time to Reflect

Do you do what you do to please the Lord, to please others, or to please yourself?

_____

Do you convince yourself of either of the lies in Ezekiel 8:12?

_____

Do you live in the awareness of how your actions and attitudes affect other people?

_____

Do you live in the reality of the constant presence of God Almighty, realizing that He is watching you?

_____

Additional Study

Proverbs 9:13–18 gives another account of this woman. Also, regarding the affects of one person on others, read Romans 5:12–19. How many did Adam's (and Eve's) wrong choice affect?

_____

And how many did Christ's action—His sacrificial death on the cross—affect?

_____

Memory Verse

Proverbs 15:3

"The eyes of the Lord are in every place, beholding the evil and the good."

Lesson Ten
A Praiseworthy Private Life

Opener

Okay, this pageant's not over yet. We still have to get a little deeper. We all know it's easy enough to be one way outside the home when other people are watching. After all, we wouldn't want them to think poorly of us. But what about inside the home where it's just us and our families?

I remember one day when I was working in a Christian daycare center, telling a four-year-old boy to *walk* to the restroom and then to *walk* back. After he left the room, I positioned myself in a corner where he couldn't see me but I could see him. Would he *walk*? Or would he run like normal?

Well, in just a few moments, here comes Ryan, RUNNING back to the classroom. I caught him. "Ryan." He stopped dead in his tracks when he heard my voice utter his name. Slowly, he turned. "Ryan, even if Mrs. Grover can't see you, God sees you," I said. He was quiet for a few moments, then with his big brown inquisitive eyes, he looked up at me and questioned, "Even when I'm at home and the doors are closed?"

"Yes. Even when you're at home and the doors are closed."

Today and tomorrow we will be taking an inside look, up close and personal, behind closed doors into the private lives of the praiseworthy pageant contestant and her problematic opponent.

Focus Passage

Read Proverbs 14:1.

Facing the Facts

How is the wise woman described (Proverbs 14:1)?

_____

Is this wise woman interested in making her home a place of encouragement and exhortation?

_____

Is she interested in making her family successful?

_____

Remember what this praiseworthy woman was doing outside the home? She was working to be able to meet the needs of her family and to be a blessing to them and others.

Do you know a New Testament term that literally means "to build up"?

_____

I think it's interesting to note that "edify" means "to build up." This wise woman builds her home. I can hardly imagine that this means without the use of encouraging words to build her family up towards godliness.

Which verse in Proverbs 31 deals with this woman's speech?

_____

Now look at another verse in Proverbs 31. Record verse 27 below.

_____

_____

_____

The opposite of looking well to the ways of her household would be idleness. Idleness is a temptation we as girls struggle with no matter what our age. After a long day at school or work, it's tempting to come home, grab a snack and a can of cola, and flop onto the La-Z-boy couch, veggin' out on our favorite TV program. That—especially if it becomes a routine rather than a once in a while occasion—is idleness!

Let's think on that word *idle*. It's the word used when you're sitting at a stoplight and your car is "idling." It might be on and running, but it's not going anywhere or doing anything until that light turns green and you put your foot back on the accelerator.

Look at the stuff this lady does inside her home: sewing, food prep, and (though not specifically mentioned, I'm sure she had our favorite household task as well . . .) cleaning. Just run your eyes through Proverbs 31:10–31.

A Closer Look

This woman is praised by her family (verse 28), and no doubt one of the reasons is the way she treats them. She's encouraging her family (verse 26). She is kind, creating an enjoyable home atmosphere. But not only that, she opens her mouth with what (verse 26)?

_____

If she opens her mouth with wisdom, she has to know what Wisdom says. How does she know what Wisdom says?

_____

What is the beginning of wisdom (Proverbs 9:10)?

_____

And it follows that since our praiseworthy model fears the Lord (Proverbs 31:30), she has gained wisdom as a result.

Read Proverbs 1:8; 6:20; and 31:1. What does a wise woman do with her wisdom?

_____

I remember as a young teen making the commitment to read my Bible every day. After a while, I really began enjoying this new part of my day. I wondered if my dad (who is one of my very best friends, by the way) spent much time reading *his* Bible. So one night when we were out on a walk, just the two of us, I asked him, not accusingly, not high-mindedly, just out of curiosity and a sincere love for his having this same joy that I was now experiencing. After sharing some of what God had been teaching me, I asked him, "Dad, do you spend time every day reading the Bible?" He didn't take offense. In fact, the Lord used that little question from a young teenage girl to invoke interest and determination. It wasn't that he never read his Bible or that he didn't love the Lord, but he admitted that because he didn't really like reading—period—he had not placed as much emphasis on this daily practice as he knew he should. Today Dad is very faithful in his time with the Lord both in Scripture-reading and prayer. He is a spiritual role model to me, in fact, and keeps me accountable. What is my point in sharing this illustration? Simply that, even as a young teenage girl, you can know wisdom and encourage your family in it. Be respectful in your approach, but know that **you can make a difference!**

Time to Reflect

Do you allow yourself to be idle at home?

_____

What time-wasters do you frequently engage in?

_____

Do you look for ways you can be an encouragement to your family at home?

_____

How do you talk to your family members inside the home, when no one else is there?

_____

When you walk into a room, do you look for what you can do to help someone else?

_____

Are you seeking wisdom for yourself so that you can share it with others?

_____

Will you choose to make a difference in your home?

_____

Additional Study

Review Proverbs 2:1–6 regarding the source of wisdom. Other verses regarding edifying fellow believers that may be helpful include Hebrews 10:22–25 and Ephesians 4:29.

Memory Verse

Proverbs 14:1

"Every wise woman buildeth her house: but the foolish plucketh it down with her hands."

Lesson Eleven
A Problematic Private Life

Opener

Are you selfish?

Say, "Whoa! That came out of nowhere." Examine yourself. Are you?

The summer between my junior and senior years in high school, I went to a leadership training camp for two weeks in North Carolina. One of the speakers handed us a nearly blank sheet of paper. We all sort of puzzled at what this was for. But after having lectured on selfishness vs. selflessness, he gave us this sheet of paper with blank lines numbered from 1 to 75.

At the top of the page, he had written "75 Ways I Am Selfish."[1] Seventy-five ways? What? I'm not *that* selfish! Oh, yeah? He told us the first few would be kind of hard, but that we'd start picking up pace and have no problem filling up the sheet . . . that, in fact, we might need a second sheet . . . or a third. He told us he didn't want us to be general. No, he wanted us to be very specific. As an example, he asked, "When you use the last piece of toilet paper on the roll, do you leave it there for the next person to get stuck with changing because he or she *needs* it, or do you change it, thinking of the next person?" Guess what became Selfish

Way #1 on my list? Yep. I failed *that* test. I began writing, and, yes, I needed a second sheet of paper.

Our second contestant, if she were honest, would need lots and lots of paper for that exercise, I'm afraid. Today we'll be looking inside her home, into her private life, and examining what she's like behind closed doors.

Focus Passage

Read Proverbs 7:11, 16–18, 27; and 21:9, 19.

Facing the Facts

How much time is this woman even at home (Proverbs 7:11)?

_____

But there are a few things mentioned that she has done in her home. What has she done inside her home according to Proverbs 7:16–17?

_____

What does she entice the young man in Proverbs 7 to come into her home to do (verse 18)?

_____

She's obviously spent time setting up a sensual atmosphere in which to temporarily quench her own selfish, lustful passions. What ultimately is her home (Proverbs 7:27)?

_____

There are lots of verses dealing with this next point, but we'll just look at two. How is this woman described in Proverbs 21:9?

_____

Is she pleasant to live with?

_____

Where would be a better place to dwell?

Where else might be an option if you were faced with having to live with this kind of person (Proverbs 21:19)?

What alternate words are used to describe her in this verse?

This woman is angry, contentious, fighting, brawling. She does not have inner peace and does not create peace for those in her presence. It comes out with the most force when she's—guess where?—at home!

Remember Proverbs 14:1 and how we reasoned that one of the ways the wise woman builds up her house is with her speech. With that picture in mind, what does this contentious, brawling, angry woman evidently do to her family with her speech (Proverbs 14:1)?

A Closer Look

In fact, these traits probably come out other places as well. Read Proverbs 27:15–16. In verse 15, what is this woman compared to?

Have you ever had a leaky roof and placed a metal bucket to catch the raindrops sneaking through? (If not, imagine you have.) Doesn't (Wouldn't) that continual "ting" of the water hitting the metal over and over and over start to drive you batty?

According to Proverbs 27:16, hiding this kind of woman is like trying to hide what?

These two verses describe this problematic pageant entrant as being so contentious that if anyone tried to hide her contentiousness, he or she would be as unsuccessful as one "trying to conceal [hide] the wind, an impossible task," or as one trying "to grasp oil with the hand. Contention, by its very nature, will show itself in some way."[2]

Have you ever tried to pick up oil with your fingers when you were baking?

A similar picture is trying to pick a piece of eggshell out of egg white with your fingers instead of with another piece of shell. It is at least this hard to cover up the fact that you are unhappy and stirring up strife.

You know, a lot of times we think we're really good at hiding our innermost feelings. But we're not. Not really. Maybe you can fool some people. But eventually not even you will be able to hide it. It'll be "written all over your face"!

Time to Reflect

Are you trying to hide something?

_____

Are you living in such a way with your family that you are a blessing to have in the house? Or would some of your family members prefer camping out in the attic or the forest as a retreat?

_____

Are you a pleasant, enjoyable addition to your family? Or do your siblings try to hang around you as little as possible?

_____

Do you need to change some things so that you don't resemble this problematic woman's behaviors and attitudes?

_____

Will you take the challenge and see if you can come up with "75 Ways I Am Selfish"?

75 Ways I Am Selfish	
1.	18.
2.	19.
3.	20.
4.	21.
5.	22.
6.	23.
7.	24.
8.	25.
9.	26.
10.	27.
11.	28.
12.	29.
13.	30.
14.	31.
15.	32.
16.	33.
17.	34.

75 Ways I Am Selfish

35.	51.
36.	52.
37.	53.
38.	54.
39.	55.
40.	56.
41.	57.
42.	58.
43.	59.
44.	60.
45.	61.
46.	62.
47.	63.
48.	64.
49.	65.
50.	66.

75 Ways I Am Selfish	
67.	72.
68.	73.
69.	74.
70.	75.
71.	

Additional Study

Try locating other verses dealing with this woman's contentiousness. Look up "contentious" in a dictionary and/or thesaurus. Then, try talking with your parents and asking them if they see any attitudes that need to change in your life.

Memory Verse

Proverbs 27:15–16a

"A continual dropping in a very rainy day and a contentious woman are alike. Whoso hideth her hideth the wind. . . ."

Lesson Twelve

A Praiseworthy and Problematic Reputation and a Final End

Opener

I have a CD of Beethoven classics. Can you guess what the final piece is?

If you guessed "Symphony No. 5 in C minor, op. 67" (better known as "Beethoven's Fifth"), you're right! It's the grand finale on this CD. Beethoven established a reputation with it. I would venture to guess that anywhere an orchestra performed selections from Beethoven's works, this Fifth Symphony would be showcased. Most of us would recognize the first four notes: da-da-da-DUM! But do you know the rest of the song? Those starting notes recur throughout the piece, but how does it *end*?

I had to pull my CD out to remind myself, though I vaguely remembered that he took a long time getting there.

It may be more challenging for us to pick up on the starting "notes" of a praiseworthy or problematic woman's lifestyle. Some things are obvious, but we cannot see the heart of anyone but ourselves.

Gradually, a recurring theme develops, a pattern is set, and a reputation is established. We've looked at the patterns of life of our two pageant contestants, but where does it end? Do you know?

Focus Passage

Read Proverbs 2:18–19; 5:3–5; 7:22–23; Galatians 5:16, 22–23; and Proverbs 31:29–31.

Facing the Facts

Look at Proverbs 2:18–19. Where does the problematic woman's path lead?

_____

Is there any return?

_____

I remember as a kid singing a song from an old video about the "point of no return." Once you've gone a certain distance, there is no turning back. Oh, yes, God can still forgive (1 John 1:9), but there are consequences and regrets that will last a lifetime.

What pictures are given in Proverbs 7:22–23 illustrating this "point of no return"?

_____

According to Proverbs 5:3, the lips of this strange woman are like what?

_____

But Proverbs 5:4 reveals this woman's end to be as bitter as what?

_____

What is her end as sharp as (Proverbs 5:4)?

_____

"On the surface, the words of the adulteress . . . are appealing, honey-coated, and smoother than oil. In reality, though, the promised pleasures leave a bitter taste in the mouth of the youth and turn into a two-edged sword that wounds no matter which way it strikes. The term 'wormwood' represents the suffering that comes from man's wickedness or from divine punishment."[1]

Not only does she bring about tragedy for the young man that she traps, but her own life ends where (Proverbs 5:5)?

Hell is a place of punishment and a state of being totally—both physically and spiritually—separated from God! I can think of NOTHING worse! NOTHING!! And she's responsible. Sure, guys are accountable for their own wrong or sinful choices, but this woman has played the temptress and lured them there, convincing them of the pleasures available, deceiving them with what are really outright lies.

Oh, girls, no matter how innocent your intent, please, *please*, PLEASE be careful how you dress, talk, and use your body! Oh, please, never let these things be said of you. Our God is too great, too wonderful for us to willfully or even ignorantly involve ourselves in this destructive path.

Don't be like the toddler who, when told not to touch something, wriggles his toes and taps the forbidden object with the tip of his big toe. There are consequences for the toddler. That toddler, gleam-in-the-eye and all, is just inviting correction—perhaps as severe as a spanking or foregoing a snack. But, oh, how much more severe the consequences for anyone party to these immoral things.

"Watch and pray, that ye enter not into temptation" (Matthew 26:41). Why? You might ask. I don't want to be like that woman. Why do I need to watch and pray if I have no desire to go that way? Read the rest of the verse (Matthew 26:41) and record what the Bible gives as the reason.

The flesh is weak. According to Galatians 5:16, what is the key to not fulfilling the lust of the flesh?

A Closer Look

And now it's time to take one final look at the praiseworthy woman's example. What, from your study so far, is this woman's reputation like?

_____

Do you think she's walking in the Spirit?

_____

What are the evidences of the Spirit's being fruitful in a person's life according to Galatians 5:22–23?

_____

Can you see these evidences in the praiseworthy woman's life?

_____

Let's go back to our highlight book of Proverbs one more time. Record Proverbs 31:29–31 below.

_____

_____

_____

_____

_____

How does that picture look? (especially compared to the ox going to the slaughter or the bird caught in a snare or trap or compared to the one in fetters or with an arrow piercing through his liver?) She's got it pretty good in the end, huh?

_____

Do you think it was easy getting there?

_____

Do you think she may have had struggles along the way?

_____

I definitely believe that she had struggles, if indeed this is talking about an actual woman and not a conglomerate ideal of a woman. Proverbs 24:16*a* says, "a just [righteous] man [person] falleth seven times [seven being the number of completion]." But what is the believer's proper response to falling?

_____

Rise up again, my friend. No matter what you've done, what you look like, or what you've been involved in, confess your sin to the appropriate persons and to the Lord; determine to forsake that way of living; memorize Scripture; make yourself accountable to someone who has been faithful (perhaps a pastor's wife or youth pastor's wife, your mom or grandma, or maybe a teacher at school); pray specifically for success; and replace the wrong with right!

The pattern according to Ephesians 4:22–24 is a three-step process. What are the three steps?

1. _____

2. _____

3. _____

Simply put: put off, renew, put on. Each step is crucial to success. You have to put off the wrong and then replace it, but in between you have to change the way you think about that wrong by studying and memorizing Scripture that will help you think the right way. Not renewing your mind is like taking your jersey off after a volleyball game and putting on clean clothes without taking a shower. On the other hand, if you put off and then renew your mind with Scriptural thinking but then fail to put a right thing in the wrong thing's place, it's like taking off your jersey, taking a shower, and then putting that sweaty, stinky jersey right back on. The practicality of the matter is, if we don't replace the rotten with the right, we'll end up putting the rotten right back on.

God never promised it would be easy, but in 1 Corinthians 10:13, He did promise that He would be _____ and that He would not allow _____
_____ .

Rise up again! You can be praiseworthy! You can be blessed! You can be fruitful! As you determine to fear the Lord (Proverbs 31:30) in all areas of your life, you will find that you will be able to "rejoice in time to come" (Proverbs 31:25). Literally, you will be able to smile at the future! What is the future for the one who fears the Lord? What is her end?

_____

Heaven—now that's something to smile about! We have a future that is secure! So, smile! Rejoice! God is not finished with you yet! He will make you beautiful in His sight! He will cause you to win this Proverbs pageant! He can, and He will . . . if you will only fear Him.

Which brings me to 1 Samuel 12:24, a verse I've claimed as my life verse: "Only fear the Lord, and serve Him in truth with all your heart: for consider how great things he hath done for you."

Time to Reflect

So, if this *were* a pageant, which woman wins?

_____

And what is the secret to her success (Proverbs 31:30)?

_____

The path you choose is up to you, but know that the consequences are pre-set and count the cost. Is sin ever worth it?

_____

Is living a life according to God's way worth it?

_____

How much of the time is living God's way worth it?

_____

Even if things get tough in this life, what do we have to look forward to as believers in Christ?

_____

And what or Who has Christ given us to help us along the way (Galatians 5:16, 22; Ephesians 5:18)?

_____

So, which path do you choose?

_____

And if you follow that path, will you become like the winner of the Proverbs pageant, a praiseworthy woman?

_____

Additional Study

You may want to study Proverbs 7:27 and 9:18; Galatians 5:16–24; Ephesians 5:1–21; and Psalm 37:23–24. It is also very interesting to study the Bible character Rahab (Rachab). In almost every passage where she is mentioned (Old and New Testaments), she is referred to as "the harlot." And yet in both Hebrews and James she is praised for her faith in action.

I would also challenge you to take one chapter of Proverbs each day for the next month and study through that chapter. I think you will find your understanding being enlightened. And I believe it will be exciting to as you find even more verses that fit into the topics we have studied in this guide.

Memory Verse

Proverbs 24:16

"For a just man falleth seven times, and riseth up again: but the wicked shall fall into mischief."

Polishing Your Reflection

Study Helps for Personal Devotions

Polishing Agents

Simply put, these are tools that you may want to use to get an even sharper reflection from the Mirror of God's Word.

Commentary

A commentary is a book that contains another person's detailed notes on a book or books of the Bible. Often, these books go verse by verse and can be used as a reference to gain insight on specific phrases or even words in a verse. My top pick for Proverbs would be Dr. Peter A. Steveson's *Commentary on Proverbs* published by BJU Press in 2001.

Concordance

Many Bibles have a simple concordance in the back of the Bible. Concordances give a list of verses that contain a specific key word. Use this to do word studies or to find a verse that you may remember a part of, but not the whole thing. The most thorough concordance (which includes all occurrences of whatever word you're studying in the King James Version) is the *Strong's Concordance*.

Cross-References

Many times as you're reading a passage you'll see a little letter superscripted next to a word or phrase that directs you to either a center or side column with references to verses other places in the Bible that would be somehow connected to the verse you are studying.

Dictionary

Using a regular dictionary is a helpful way to make sure you understand what the words of Scripture mean. There are also Bible dictionaries that can give you a little more detailed definition of what that word would have meant in Bible times.

Thesaurus

Using a thesaurus, like a dictionary, can be helpful in giving a fuller understanding of the word. A thesaurus won't give a definition but will give you synonyms for the word you're studying.

Translation

Looking up the word in another good translation of Scripture may also be a tool to discover synonyms or to get a fuller grasp on what a particular verse or phrase means.

How Do I Look?

This is not so much what you see, but with what attitude you choose to look. The following heart attitudes will help you get a more accurate picture of yourself as you look in the Mirror.

Honesty

Be willing to admit your struggles. Be totally honest with yourself and before the Lord. He already knows everything anyway. We can't hide from Him. Truly, in studying the Bible, as in all of life, "honesty is the best policy."

Willingness to Change

Having a heart that is willing to make changes is the only way to spiritual success. You can't kick against the pricks and expect to grow from them at the same time. Accept what God is doing in your life. Be willing for Him to work on you.

Determination

This is a must if you are to tackle a project. You will come to bumps in the road, hills, and sometimes even foreboding mountains. But be determined to dig and climb and tackle the task. It will be worth it in the end. Know that all along the way, God is with you and wants you to learn and grow in the knowledge and understanding of Him.

Seeing Clearly

This deals with proper interpretation as you look at a passage.

Context

Make sure you take verses in context, not trying to make them say what you'd like them to say, but taking them for what they were intended to say. This may mean backing up and reading a few more verses or even a chapter or two, but the time invested will be worth it.

Literal Interpretation

Take what the Bible says at face value. Don't try to spiritualize straightforward truths. This will make your Bible study much easier and more enjoyable as well as more accurate and profitable.

Agents for Change

Unlike makeup's change on our faces (very temporary), implementing the following will help change our lives from the inside out forever.

Meditation

Think about the things you've been studying throughout your day. Just stop and take the time to consider how those truths practically apply to you.

Questioning

This is closely linked with meditation, perhaps a strategy on how to begin meditating. As in the "Facing the Facts" section, when you study through a passage, get the details down. Find out the facts of what's going on—the old "Who, What, Where, When, How" list is helpful. Then as you're ready for "A Closer Look," ask the "Why" question.

Memorization

Scripture memory is a key to winning the spiritual battle. Those verses are your weapons against Satan.

Personalization

Take "Time to Reflect." Whenever you read your Bible, personalize it. Ask God to show you how what you are reading applies to your life.

Prayer

Prayer is vital to any studying in the Bible. It is the Spirit that gives enlightenment, shines the light on truth, and makes it real to you.

Accountability

Perhaps the greatest help to you as you work on mastering Scripture will be an accountability partner. This can be a friend, parent, teacher, or other person you respect. Knowing someone is going to be checking on you can really help you stay committed to changing a habit or conquering a temptation.

Remembering What You Saw

Meditation and memorization could almost fit under this category as well, but here are a few extra things that will help you to remember the reflection you saw in God's Mirror and not be like the "forgetful hearer" in James 1 that "beholdeth himself, and goeth his way, and straightway forgetteth what manner of man he was" (verse 24). Instead, if you will remember and act on what you saw, you will "be blessed in [your] deed" (James 1:25).

Journaling

Whether it's recording answers or copying out a verse, there's something about writing that gets information into our brains more concretely than if we just read it or hear it. Even though it takes extra time, it's well worth the effort.

Review

It's always good to review what you've studied in the past. Keep this study guide and any other spiritual journals together in a special place where you can get to them and pull them out easily and review from time to time. You'll be amazed at the process of growth God has brought you through.

Action

Take action on what you saw. Make an effort to change any blemishes in your reflection. By the grace of God, be a "doer" of the Word (James 1:23, 25).

Sure or Unsure
Knowing Where You Will Spend Eternity

Did you ever see those deodorant advertisements on television for the brand "Sure"? Remember how the people were either holding their arms tightly to their sides, trying to prevent any odor from wafting out from the pit, or how they were holding their arms confidently up in the air after completing some major athletic competition? It was all to illustrate a truth: Deodorant is an important part of our daily adult lives.

Deodorant is important, but so much more important is our individual assurance of salvation. Assurance is eternally more important than Sure. It matters that we not stink when we're with our friends or coworkers. But it matters more that we not "stink" in the nostrils of God.

Are you sure . . . spiritually? Are you confident when a pastor or evangelist asks for a raise of hands of all those that know for sure they are on their way to heaven? Can you raise your hand without a shadow of a doubt?

First, let's make sure we understand what salvation is. Salvation is not merely walking an aisle or saying a prayer. It is the commencement of a personal relationship with God in which we realize our need for a Savior from our sin and our dependence upon Him for eternal life. It is a confessing of our sins and a claiming of His grace and favor as He has promised He would give to those who believe on His name. If you are questioning whether or not you have ever placed your faith in Christ alone for salvation, I would encourage you to get with a counselor who understands and knows God's Word.

Second, many people struggle with assurance of salvation. The key here is not the answer to these questions: "Did I have enough faith?" "Did I say the right thing?" "Did I really mean it when I prayed?" Rather it is the answer to the question, "Who or what am I trusting for eternal salvation?" It is not so much about us as it is totally and completely about Christ. It is not the amount of faith but the object that our faith is in. If we are trusting in our own works to save us, we have no hope. But if our faith is in Christ, no matter how small our faith is, Christ is our confident hope and expectation, and we can rejoice in the promises of His Word.

The following are some verses that you may want to memorize and claim to combat the devil's fiery darts of doubt that he will try to launch at you. God's Word is our Sword, and faith in It is our Shield!

Romans 3:23

Romans 6:23

Ephesians 2:8–9

Romans 5:8

Romans 10:9–10

Romans 8:1

John 15:16

Endnotes

Lesson Five

[1]R.C.H. Lenski, *Commentary on the New Testament: The Interpretation of St. Paul's Epistles to the Colossians, to the Thessalonians, to Timothy, to Titus, and to Philemon* (Peabody, MA: Hendrickson, 2001), p. 559.

[2]Lenski, p. 559.

Lesson Six

[1]Peter A. Steveson, *A Commentary on Proverbs* (Greenville, SC: BJU Press, 2001), p. 97.

[2]Steveson, p. 98.

[3]Steveson, p. 98.

Lesson 9

[1]Steveson, p. 96.

[2]Quoted by Dr. Gordon A. Dickson, Calvary Baptist Church, Findlay, OH.

Lesson 11

[1]Used by Jim Berg in the Camper In Training Program at The WILDS, Brevard, NC, Summer 1998.

[2]Steveson, p. 381.

Lesson 12

[1]Steveson, p. 68.

Bibliography

Dillow, Linda. *Calm My Anxious Heart: A Woman's Guide to Finding Contentment.* Colorado Springs: NavPress, 1998.

George, Elizabeth. *Beautiful in God's Eyes: The Treasures of the Proverbs 31 Woman.* Eugene, OR: Harvest House, 1998.

-----. *A Woman's High Calling: 10 Essentials for Godly Living.* Eugene, OR: Harvest House, 2001.

Laird, Charlton, et al. *Webster's New World Thesaurus.* 3rd ed. New York: Macmillan, 1997.

Lenski, R. C. H. *Commentary on the New Testament: The Interpretation of St. Paul's Epistles to the Colossians, to the Thessalonians, to Timothy, to Titus, and to Philemon.* Peabody, MA: Hendrickson, 2001.

MacArthur, John Jr. *Different by Design: Discovering God's Will for Today's Man and Woman.* Colorado Springs: Chariot Victor Press, 1994.

Steveson, Peter A. *A Commentary on Proverbs.* Greenville, SC: BJU Press, 2001.

Webster, Merriam. *Merriam Webster's Collegiate Dictionary.* 10th ed. Springfield, MA: Merriam-Webster, 1993.

About the Author

At 24, Michelle Grover has recently been "the girl in the mirror" and remembers the challenges and pressures of being a teenager. As a teen, she lettered in volleyball and track, enjoyed piano and flute, and got some practical work experience both baby-sitting and as a crew leader at McDonald's. Since that time she has graduated from BJU with a major in special education and married her college sweetheart, Alan Grover. She is now the mother of a growing family and has worked with teens in schools, Christian camps, and church youth groups.

"Looking in a mirror can confront a teen girl with all kinds of questions," says Michelle. "But, thankfully, when the Mirror she uses is God's Word, that girl can find the answers she's looking for!"